The Masterpiece
A Pre-Ramble of the Glories of Jesus
Christ in the Everyman!

Written by: Matt Spinks
Illustrated by: Gordon Johnson

(This book is meant as an illustrated pre-release
to the full length book, *God's Perfect
Masterpiece,* by Matt Spinks. Coming soon!)

This book is dedicated to the masterpieces in my
home, Katie Rose, Samuel, and Rainbow Glory!

Published by:
The Fire House Ministries & Publications
12222 US Highway 30 E New Haven, IN 46774
www.thefirehouseprojects.com
Email: info@thefirehouseprojects.com

WELCOME TO THE NEW CREATION!

The Glory of God
is a HUMAN
fully alive...

St. Irenaeus of Lyons

"**For we are**
God's masterpiece
**Created anew in Christ
Jesus so we can do the
GOOD things planned for
us long ago.**"

St. Paul to the Ephesians

Is God an Artist?

Is God an Artist?

16
Kl.4

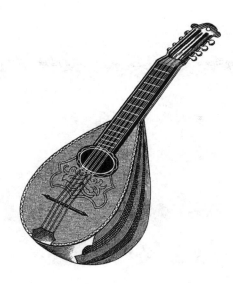

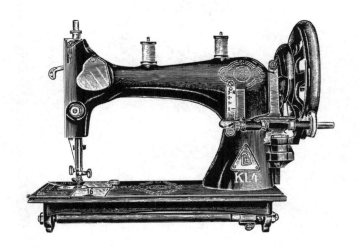

Do you ever feel like
God is...

...asking too much
hard to please
narcisisstic
not a good leader person
a perfectionist
distant
closed off
cold
judgy
just not good?

I saw the Light.
I saw the Light...

Once upon a time...

...in the early 2000s, I discovered the Finished Work of Jesus Christ...

It wasn't just a message, but a living glowing unfolding reality that carried with it a tangible life change. I began to see WHY JESUS DIED on the cross, and what it accomplished for this not-so-random guy two thousand years later...

I had been a passionate spiritual person all my life, but never had I found something (SomeOne) with so much empowering mystical substance!

The message was simple, yet utterly transforming. It was not complex, yet neither was it shallow.

Simply put, in the Person of Jesus, I saw all of heaven and earth come together! All of God and all of humanity were united in Him! I saw this as already completed, once and for all.

When He died on that cross, on the hill of Golgotha in Jerusalem, everything that was never truly me, every last stitch of it, died too.

Then, He was raised!!! And, I began to realize that I was raised with Him! Every thing that I ever truly wanted to be, even greater than my wildest dreams, I became that person! The powerful Love dream that had gotten messed up in the corruption, greed, selfishness, and violence of this world... all of this was restored! Oh, and there was so much more!!!

Personally, I had been quite the critical, judgmental, and proud person before this. Oh, most of my friends and family would have said that I was a "very good person." But, those close to me... I only burned them out through a standard that was never achievable.

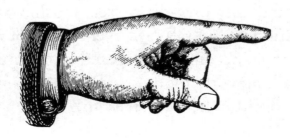

The Message of what Christ actually accomplished on the cross removed all of the scales. Both the scales on my eyes to the beauty of all creation, and the scales of perfectionistic measurement; they all fell away!

I began to see myself and others as complete, whole, BEAUTIFUL! The work of Christ had healed us all! The Person of Christ was preserving us all, on earth, even as we are in heaven.

My actual days began to FEEL like heaven on earth!

I saw that anything truly negative had been absorbed into Him, and it died with Him through His death. All that was now left was goodness! And, it was His goodness! The experience of feeling this warm life-giving pure and holy love-drunk relationship with a relational God satisfied every sense of my emotional neediness. I began the adventure of walking with my Beloved, Abba, Jesus, & Holy Spirit in heaven on earth!

That adventure continues to this day...

I'm living in unhindered access to life and Glory because of what Jesus Christ did... once and for all!

And, the people around me are thanking Him for it too! LOL!

Hallelujah!

what kind of art would God make?

The Loving Master Artist...

What we say about the quality of a person's work directly reflects on them AS a person. In this little book we're exploring the nature of the actual quality of life that is given through Jesus Christ and his work. The aim is that readers will be awakened to Father, Son, and Holy Spirit, as the beautiful Master Artist that They are, and we, Their perfect masterpiece!

If we are the creations of God, then what we say about ourselves directly reflects back on our Creator. We say that God is Love. We say that God is all-powerful. Does our view of what He's done reflect that? Is our life in the day to day a testament to a beautiful Master Artist? Maybe it IS, more than we know!?!

The Finished Work of Jesus Christ is a view that is coming with more and more clarity in these days. It presents a comprehensive Gospel of all humanity being included in the life of the Trinity, through Jesus and what He accomplished eternally in time some two thousand plus years ago.

The Finished Work presents a spiritual Path that glorifies the beauty of Abba, Jesus, and Holy Spirit because it actually works, revealing Their creation as a flawless masterpiece! What Jesus has done has made us much, much greater than Michaelangelo's *David*, Beethoven's *Moonlight Sonata*, yes, all of the greatest works of art this world has ever known!

Of course, all this is dependent upon Him, so there's no room for self-centered boasting!

The scriptures surely testify to the fact that we lost our way, choosing selfishness, and horribly marring the masterpiece through sin. However, the Master Themself chose to step into Their creation to restore and redeem. In a profound mystery, God worked all things for our good, weaving us, and even our mistakes, into something more beautiful than we were to begin with!

This is the reality of the Finished Work of Jesus Christ displayed in this little book. This is the true story of how our human lives have been restored to sublime beauty and actual glory in real day to day life!

Some would call this salvation, sanctification, healing, restoration, redemption, or glorification even...

All of that happened in the coming of our Master and Savior, Jesus Christ! And, all of that is COMPLETE! It's a done deal. There will be nothing greater than the masterpiece that Jesus Christ accomplished in His Person & work! We have everything we need to live an incredible full life now through our life giving union with Him!

"It is Finished!"
- Jesus of Nazareth -

For whom he did foreknow, he also did predestinate
to be conformed to the image of his Son,
that he might be the firstborn among many brethren.
Moreover whom he did predestinate,
them he also called and whom he called,
them he also justified and whom he justified,
them he also glorified.

St. Paul to the Romans

DID somEone sAy
lIfE GIVING UNIOn?

I AM IN YOU!

YOU ARE IN ME!

And, behold I saw a flawless sailing vessel...

Take a moment...

... and try to visualize in your head a big beautiful sail boat, something like an old time schooner or a large sailing yacht. Now imagine this boat is the greatest ship ever made in the history of the world, by far! This beautiful ship is you, me, us, humanity.

Much of the church today would imagine that this vessel is actually quite broken, extremely flawed. They would say that it has potential. "It has some potential, but things do look pretty bleak. It's got a lot of rot going on in the underbelly with many damaged parts. Maybe with a lot of work it could get cleaned up. It's possible, though it will never really fully sail properly, not in this lifetime, not until long after this set of sailors passes on anyways."

"We should try our best to sail it anyways, using the help of the guy who built it as much as we can, and hopefully we can try to make some improvements as we go. Someday the builder will return and make this vessel whole."

"The best thing about this ship right now," they say, "is that it's been declared to be worth a whole lot! The ship builder who created it is telling everyone that it's perfect. The ship builder himself even sees it as perfect."

"So, we don't want to give up on this boat, even though everyone else who sees it and all the sailors on it know for sure it won't but barely make it to the next island over. The ship-builder is, however, going to reward these sailors handsomely someday for continuing to sail it their whole lives the best they can."

"Every now and then they will even be able to tune their ship radio in for advice from the master builder. This ship radio is pretty difficult to use though, so the sailors often get lost and confused along the way.

The ship is in such bad shape really, so the sailors mostly keep it in port attempting to make continual repairs. Only a few super sailors have ever had much success with the boat, or so their stories go."

But, what if there was another COMPLETELY different story to this beautiful sailing schooner!?!

Back to visualizing something like the greatest sailing yacht of all time...

The master builder has taken every measure to make this vessel flawless from top to bottom. He not only believes that it's perfect, it actually is. It's also not just the best ship ever made, it's made of indestructible materials!

This ship's materials have also been infused with the kind of divine substance that could only come from the master himself. It's a boat like nothing ever seen before! The master builder has also personally imparted his knowledge into it's sailors, who are literally members of his own family. They will be sailing the ship, under the direct command of the master builder. The best part is that the master builder travels with the ship wherever it goes!

SOME OLD TYPES
of
SHIPS.

SAXON. HAROLD'S SHIP

NORMAN— WILLIAM'S SHIP

1240. HENRY III

14. Cent.

1460

1200. JOHN

GREAT HARRY— 1514
Henry VIII

17th. Cent.y

DUKE OF YORK'S
PLEASURE BOAT

DUKE OF YORK'S SHIP— 1661

1680

The master builder is the captain. He is a sailor himself. He's spent considerable time in a vessel just like this one and has mastered the art of sailing it, specifically.

The whole crew is therefore obviously of the utmost confidence. This vessel is ready to set out on any journey with great joy! The whole team has the pleasure of adventuring on the water, discovering new lands, enjoying the comradery.

They surely encounter storms and troubles as they adventure, but there is always an incredible confidence in the quality of the vessel and the team that is sailing it. And, after many adventures the whole crew realizes that there was such an ease in the adventuring because the master-builder had already sailed this ship through these waters long before!

There's an ease...

In the Breeze...

Do you ever feel like you are ...

...a wreck

a mess

broken

beyond repair

full of flaws

missing out

not measuring up

not enough

screwed over

just not good?

Neither selfish, nor victims...

How many times...

...have you encountered some struggle within yourself, or in someone else in your life, and it feels insurmountable? It's as if they are broken. It's as if you are flawed by design.

How many times have you encountered selfishness in this world? In yourself? Isn't it exhausting? Tiring? Disgusting, right? And, yet most of us have come to accept this. Oh, we may judge everyone for it, and many times we certainly do, but we still think it's all there is.

We have so many different ways of saying it.
"It's just human nature."
"We're all sinful." "We're all broken."
"No one is perfect." "We all have flaws!"

Both the world, and the church, have normalized brokenness. We have normalized selfishness. For the most part we have given up, as a people, on the idea of actually being free from ego.

You know, "ego." I'm talking about that fake part of us that has identified with selfishness and self preservation rather than the loving person we want to be. I mean, even the preachers don't live it, right?

Long story short... I'm convinced that there is more! I've tasted and seen! We CAN actually love each other! People can live free from ego and selfishness!

I've met folks AND experienced it for myself. It is very possible to live in a new child-like identity by the power of the Spirit of Christ.

It's not by our efforts, which only produce more pride in our own "ego" abilities, and that "holier than thou" vibe that is so disgusting.

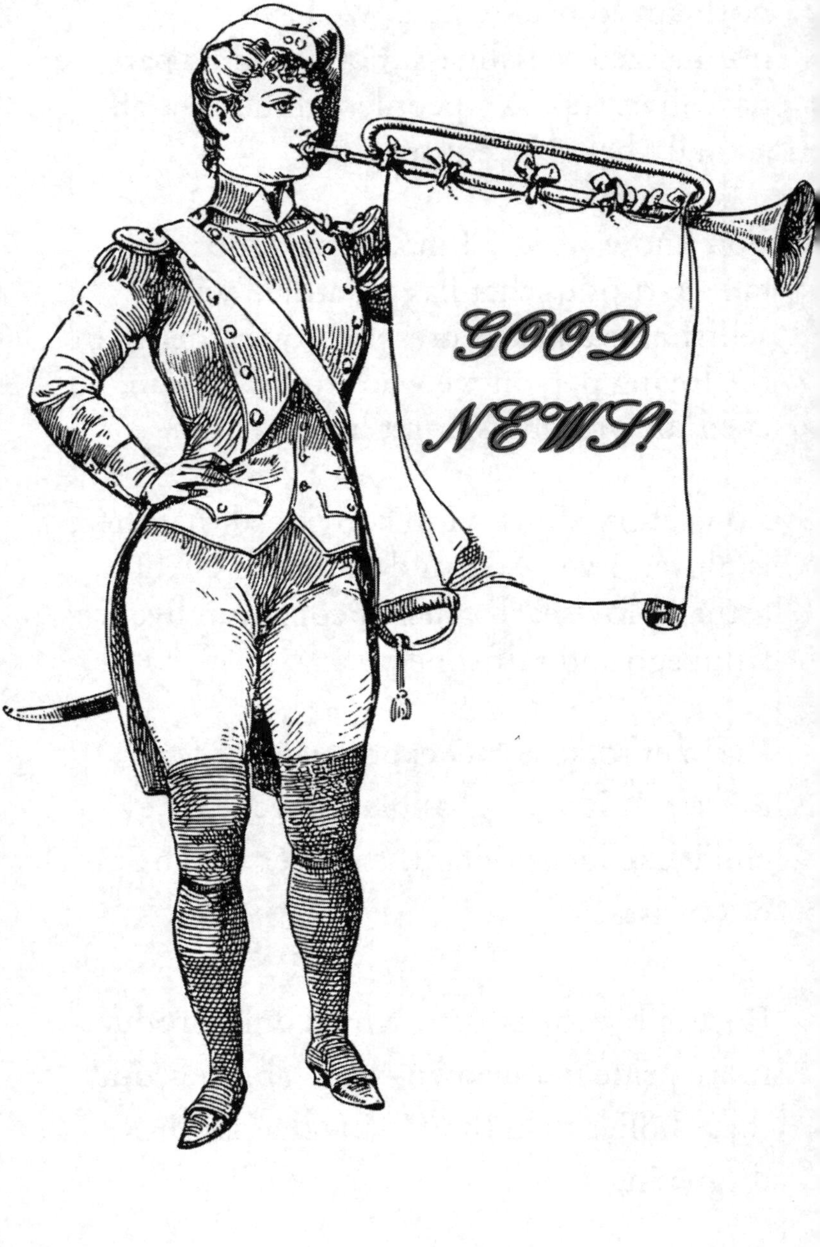
GOOD
NEWS!

It's NOT by a long process that never ends, except maybe after we die, NO! What would that help in this life anyways? Why would God leave us bound up for any amount of time?

No, nothing like that! Our freedom comes from a simple awareness that Jesus has ALREADY cleansed and healed us. He alone, by His one saving act, has restored us to ourselves. Jesus enacted a new creation, both renewed to our original state, and given us an ecstatically better-than-ever-before state!

He has rescued us from our selfish sickness, COMPLETELY WHOLE!

This doesn't mean we won't make mistakes from time to time. It does mean that we have re-identified with who we really are in Him. And, it produces fruit. Kindness, love, child-likeness, patience are our actual nature!

Can you imagine if the whole world was walking free from selfishness and ego?!?!

OH GOD, the greatest part of what Jesus has done! That and giving us perfect union relationship with God and one another; these two are absolutely connected!

To begin to live in this, we simply must see what God knows to be true about us in union with Him.

The revelation of the scriptures must begin to hold more weight than our personal beliefs, our experiences, and the popular voices of our day. Jesus defines us, nothing else! For real, in our thought life, and at our core, His reality must be our vision!

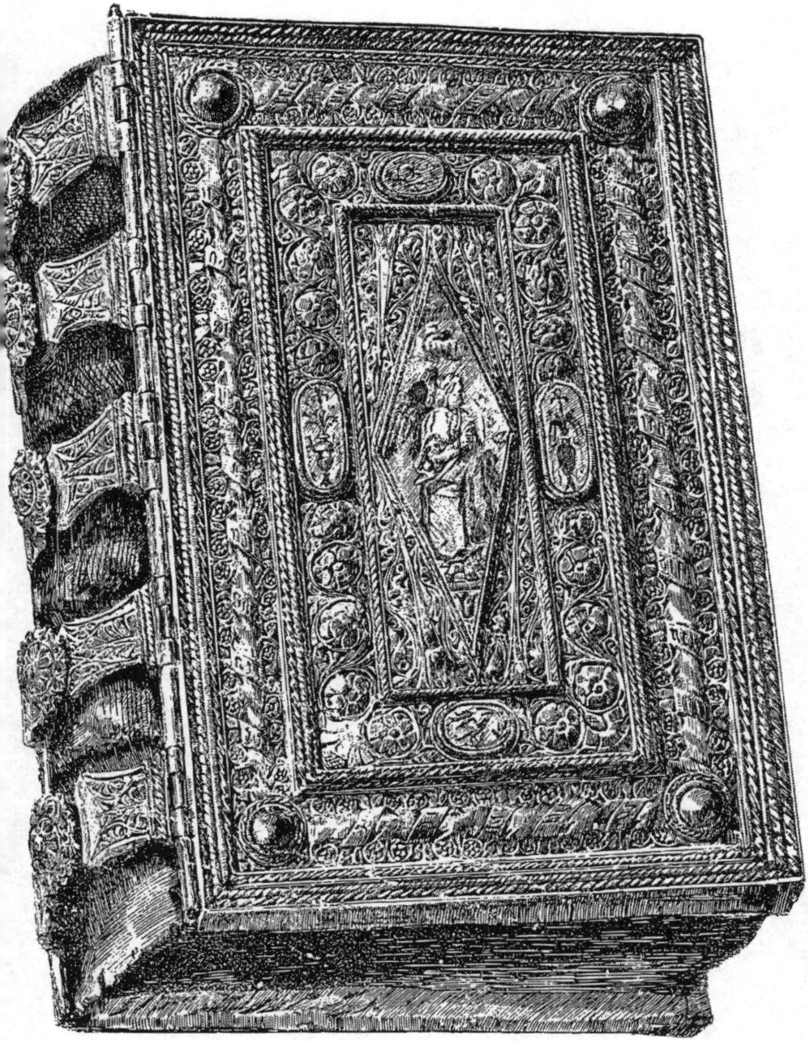

"For by a single offering he has made the sanctified perfect for all time." - Hebrews 10:14

"No one born of God makes a practice of sinning, for God's seed abides in him, and he cannot keep on sinning because he has been born of God." - 1 John 3:9

"And you are in Him, made full and having come to fullness of life [in Christ you too are filled with the Godhead--Father, Son and Holy Spirit--and reach full spiritual stature]. And He is the Head of all rule and authority [of every angelic principality and power]." - Colossians 2:10

You are altogether beautiful, my love; there is no flaw in you.

- Song of Solomon 4:7 -

"For if, because of one man's trespass, death reigned through that one man, much more will those who receive the abundance of grace and the free gift of righteousness reign in life through the one man Jesus Christ. Therefore, as one trespass led to condemnation for all men, so one act of righteousness leads to justification and life for all men. For as by the one man's disobedience the many were made sinners, so by the one man's obedience the many will be made righteous." - Romans 5:17-19

Scriptures like these reveal the truth of what Jesus has done for us! This is what changed my life forever!

As those truths became lodged in my mind, I no longer saw myself as flawed, selfish, broken, or struggling! And, I no longer saw anyone else that way either.

I can not describe how life changing this revelation is!

It inspires confidence, and trust. Not in my SELF. But, in the Spirit of Christ in union with me to continuously inspire me to make the best choices! For, it's only by Christ within that I can live ego-free.

Yet, this is not something that requires my ongoing assistance to maintain. I've been THERE too, and it's only exhausting.

If it depends on me, then I become proud when I succeed, and condemned when I fail. And, it's just a lot of work TRYING to be what I already am!

Freedom from selfishness comes when the focus on "I" is completely gone!

The apostle Paul, the great preacher of Grace, said it this way:

"I am crucified with Christ: nevertheless I live; yet not I, but Christ liveth in me: and the life which I now live in the flesh I live by the faith of the Son of God, who loved me, and gave himself for me." - Galatians 2:20

"Yet not I!" What a powerful phrase! The "I" there in the Greek is "ego!" The "I" was crucified with Christ! That's why Jesus died! He didn't die his own death! He died our death! He took our false selfish self to the grave once and for all. When Jesus died, He took the ego of all humanity with Him!

Christ

carries us

along the way...

This is the joy of my life now!
I feel His virtue living within my core!
My old selfish self is completely gone!

It feels so good to only feel LOVE coming
from inside me! It's a real tangible
experience every day now. And, it works...

I'm no longer waiting for some future day
when I can live free and full of love for all.
This is the glorious truth of my life, and I
continue to share it with others.

It isn't a big complicated journey.
Jesus did it! Once and for all!!

You are not broken.
You are not stuck.
Your ego died with Jesus!
We are not victims, but happy powerful
super natural children of God!

† WE ARE GOD'S MASTERPIECE! †

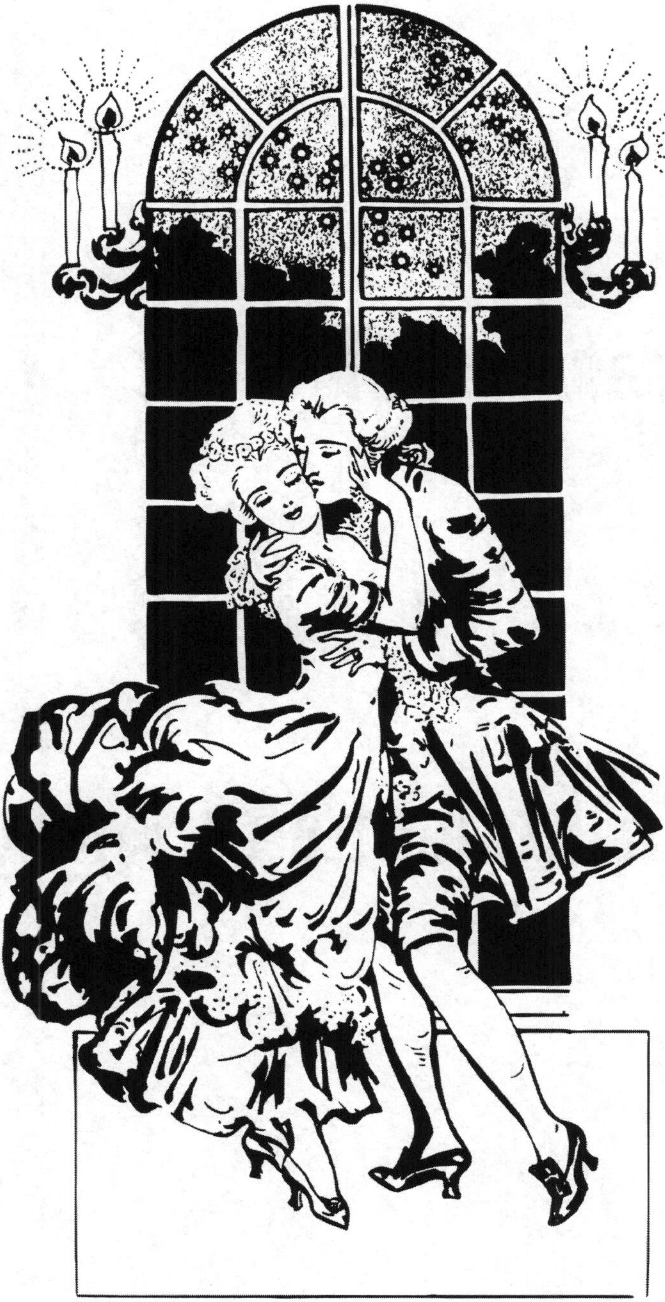

Man is fully alive
in
the vision of God.

St. Irenaeus of Lyons

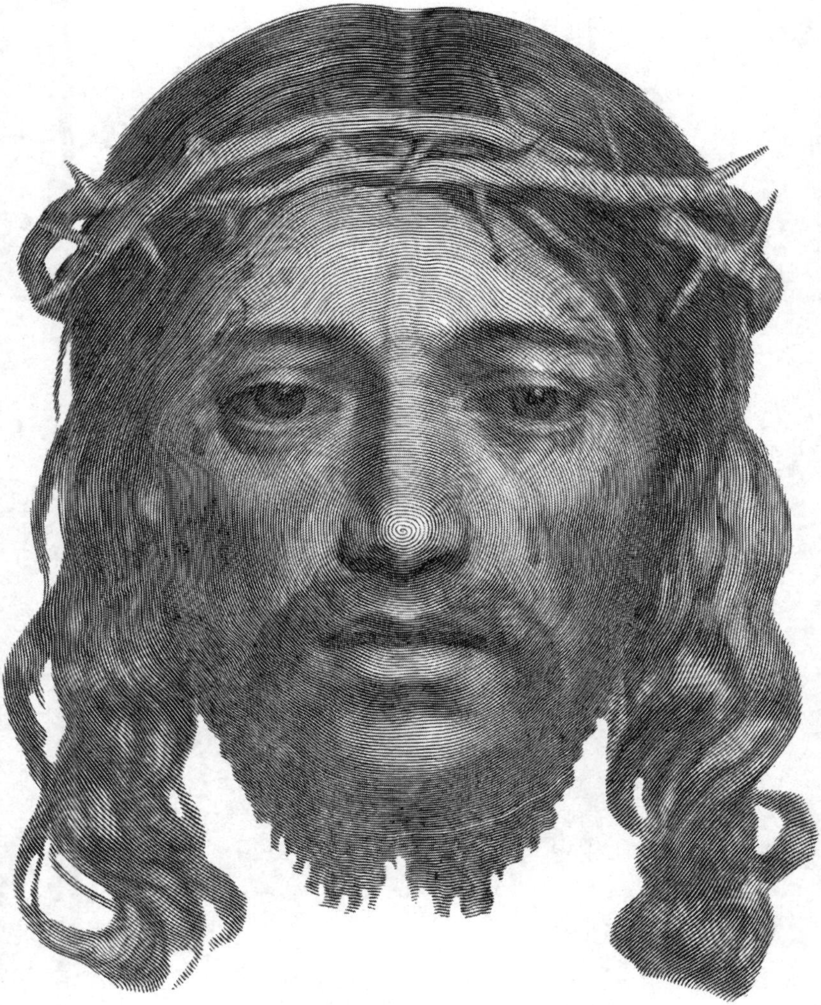

We Are a nEW creaTiOn!